This book belongs to

____

Courtney Crumrin

Volume One

The Night Things

Courtney Crumrin

Volume One

The Night Things

Written & Illustrated by

TED NAIFEH

Colored by

WARREN WUCINICH

Original Series edited by

JAMES LUCAS JONES

Collection edited by

JILL BEATON

Design by

KEITH WOOD

Oni Press, Inc.

publisher, Joe Nozemack

editor in chief, James Lucas Jones

director of marketing, Cory Casoni

art director, Keith Wood

operations director, George Rohac

editor, Jill Beaton

editor, Charlie Chu

digital prepress lead, Troy Look

Originally published as issues 1-4 of the Oni Press comic series *Courtney Crumrin and the Night Things.*

Courtney Crumrin and the Night Things, April 2012. Published by Oni Press, Inc. 1305 SE Martin Luther King Jr. Blvd., Suite A, Portland, OR 97214.

1305 SE Martin Luther King Jr. Blvd.
Suite A
Portland, OR 97214

www.onipress.com

First Edition: April 2012

ISBN 978-1-934964-77-4

1 3 5 7 9 10 8 6 4 2

Library of Congress Control Number: 2011933140

Printed in China.

To Magic, for helping awaken my imagination, and to Ron,
for telling me of the Night Things.

A Few Words About Children, Nightmares, And Outcasts

Childhood is a much darker world than most adults care to remember. If anything, childhood is even more full of terror and passion than life becomes after a few decades spent killing off brain cells. Small children are straight outta nature, all id, tribal survivalists to the core. They drive the weak away from the village, instinctively hating those who are different, ugly, or slow. Sure, they're preoccupied with stockpiling toys instead of guns, but the principle is always the same. Behind the big shiny eyes and dimples is The Lord of the Flies, ticking and buzzing. We learn sweetness and the ability to sit still later on in order to fit into society and get grown-up things like jobs and apartments and girl- or boyfriends, things that seem yucky and boring until the moment we're ready for them. Among the byproducts that boil off and are lost in the process of growing up are simplicity, lots of dreams, and a huge amount of fear.

Children understand fear. But there are also childhood terrors that go even deeper than the social torture experienced daily in every grammar school in the world. One of the worst nightmares I ever had seemed to be trying to explain the bedtime fears that all kids go through. While I was asleep, my brain told me a story about children and their common, silly childhood fears: the dark, the bogeyman, the creature in the closet, the monster under the bed. The stuff we learn to laugh at and later humor and comfort in our own children. Then I saw the human predators, the real-life monsters such as serial killers and child murderers, and their helpless prey. My mind suggested that it was the terror suffered by these victims that, via some kind of collective unconscious, shows up as the Thing at the Foot of the Bed. That even the most sheltered kid lovingly tucked in every night somehow knows about these very real bogeymen and feels the horror of the unlucky ones, the ones who got caught. At 4 a.m. I woke up screaming and sat with all the lights on and my back to the wall until the watery winter sun came up. I'd never been so glad to be an adult before.

Strangely enough, despite all of the more or less real terrors they contend with on a daily and nightly basis, children love to be scared, love to be grossed out, love, above all, to be shocked.

The only children's stories that are truly classic, timeless, and beloved are also subversively honest about life's ugliness. Kids experience reality on a much simpler level than adults, and don't buy stories that are too sugary. They're realists in the sense that they know there's much more to reality than what we see around us every day or what we learn in school. There almost has to be a tragic, a bitter, or a vicious edge to the story, or they know it for the load of bull it is. Mark Twain, Roald Dahl, and Judy Blume, three of the all-time best-beloved children's authors, knew this. Their books are often banned from schools and libraries because of parents' need to believe that children are innocent of pain and cruelty and can be protected from knowledge about the darkness of human nature.

I grew up on those and other great authors, whose books gave me a glimpse at life's beautiful and horrible truths. Now that I'm an adult, at least in the sense that I have to pay taxes and worry about gingivitis, I see that I'm a part of the diaspora of kids that was driven from the village, for various reasons, and spent adolescence observing it all from the outside. We've formed our own tribes, and as far as I can see, we, the geeks, won. We're smarter, we're independent, we're more courageous, and we value each other more than the kids who fit in without effort, blending in and never really getting to know themselves. I only wish I could tell my little sister, who's about Courtney's age, and rapidly moving from the unicorn stage to the moody poetry stage and reading everything she can get her hands on, to hang in there. Sure, it'll be a rough eight or ten years, but at the end of it, she'll be a conscious, brilliant, confident woman with a loving, like-minded community and her own unique style. It's worth the pain you feel now. Trust me. And grown-up geekboys do make the best partners. I should know.

Actually, come to think of it, that doesn't sound particularly comforting—eight years is a lifetime to a kid. And of course, you can't tell kids anything.

—Kelly Crumrin, Fall 2002

Kelly Crumrin is a freelance writer who lives in San Francisco and would head the campaign to elect Emperor Norton as president if only he weren't so dead.

CAREFUL NOW.
OLD PROFESSOR CRUMRIN DON'T TAKE KINDLY TO YOUNGSTERS GALLY-VANTIN' IN 'IS BACK-YARD.

I SEE EVERTHIN' WHAT GOES ON 'ROUND 'ERE.
I'M THE NEIGHBORHOOD'S OLDEST RESIDENT.
NAME'S BUTTERWORM.

I SAW CRUMRIN HOUSE BUILT.
IT WERE THE FIRST HOUSE IN 'ILLSBOROUGH, BEFORE IT BECOME A POSH NEIGHBORHOOD FULL 'A SPOILT LITTLE BRATS.

I HEAR 'EM TALKIN', THE LITTLE DEVILS.
HEAR ALL THEM NASTY RUMORS. AX MURDERS IN THE ATTIC.
THAT LAD MICHAEL JACKSON COMING OUT EVERY YEAR TO GET HIS NOSE FIXED UP.
THEY LIVE IN MORTAL TERROR O' THE OLD PLACE, BLESS 'EM.

I'LL TELL YEH THIS FER NOTHIN'.
ALL THEM RUMORS?

COMPARED WITH WHAT REALLY GOES ON IN THERE, ALL THAT'S JUST A SPLASH IN THE KIDDIE-POOL.

Chapter One

DO YOU KNOW THAT LITTLE BOROUGH OUTSIDE THE CITY, THE ONE WITH ALL THE BIG MANSIONS AND TREES?
DO YOU KNOW THAT ONE HOUSE, THE MOST TALKED ABOUT HOUSE IN THE WHOLE NEIGHBORHOOD?

NOT THE FANCY MARBLE-COLUMNED OUDLER MANSION, NOR RADLEY HALL WHERE PRESIDENT NIXON ONCE DINED IN THE SEVENTIES. NO, I'M REFERRING TO THE HOUSE OF OLD ALOYSIUS CRUMRIN.

IT IS WELL KNOWN THAT TERRIBLE THINGS HAPPEN THERE, AND THAT OLD MAN CRUMRIN IS MADDER THAN A VICTORIAN HATMAKER.

WELL, THAT'S THE HOUSE THAT COURTNEY CRUMRIN WOULD SOON BE CALLING HOME.

UNCLE ALOYSIUS WAS GETTING ON IN YEARS, AND WOULD SOON NEED LOOKING AFTER.
...AND COURTNEY'S PARENTS WERE RUNNING OUT OF CREDIT CARDS, SO THE CHANCE TO LIVE RENT-FREE IN A WEALTHY SUBURB WAS TOO GOOD TO PASS UP.

SHE HAD BEEN TO THE HOUSE BEFORE AS A YOUNG CHILD.
HER MEMORIES OF IT WERE NOT PLEASANT ONES.
THE DISREPAIR AND GENERAL GLOOM OF THE PLACE ONLY ADDED TO HER APPREHENSION.

THE LOWER FLOORS ARE YOURS...
BUT DON'T YOU DARE STICK YOUR NOSES IN MY PRIVATE CHAMBERS.

HE SHOT HER A WITHERING GAZE WITH HIS TERRIBLE EYES.
WOULD YOU CARE FOR SOME HOT COCOA?

NO, THANK YOU, SIR.
UNCLE ALOYSIUS WAS EVEN NASTIER THAN SHE REMEMBERED HIM, WITH A FACE THAT WOULD CURDLE NEW MILK.
THE PROSPECT OF LIVING UNDER HIS ROOF BEGAN TO SINK IN THEN, AND COURTNEY'S STOMACH TURNED TO ICEWATER.
"I MUST HAVE BEEN REALLY ROTTEN IN MY PREVIOUS LIFE," THOUGHT COURTNEY.
"MAYBE A GYM TEACHER."

HER ROOM WAS COLD, DUSTY AND COMFORTLESS. COURTNEY DEALT WITH HER DISAPPOINTMENT THE BEST WAY SHE KNEW HOW...
...GRUMBLE...

IT WAS DIFFICULT TO SLEEP, FOR THE COVERS SMELLED OF AGE, AND THE HOUSE'S TIMBERS EMITTED STRANGE CREAKS AND GROANS.

BUT MORE ALARMING BY FAR WAS THE SOUND OF SOMETHING STIRRING AT THE FOOT OF HER BED.
WHO'S THERE!?!

AT FIRST SHE COULDN'T REMEMBER WHERE SHE WAS.
BUT AS WAKEFULNESS TOOK HOLD, A SINGLE STRAY DREAM SEEMED TO REMAIN.

CONFUSED THOUGHTS STRUGGLED IN HER SLEEPY MIND TO EXPLAIN WHAT SHE WAS SEEING.

IT WASN'T TILL SHE HAD THE LIGHT ON THAT ICY PANIC BEGAN TO TAKE HOLD.
HUH ...

NEEDLESS TO SAY, SHE DIDN'T CLOSE HER EYES AGAIN ALL NIGHT. WOULD YOU?

ARTUAD, AXEL?
PRESENT.

BLOOM, BELINDA?
PRESENT.
CRUMRIN, COURTNEY?

YEAH.

YOUNG LADY, THE PROPER RESPONSE IS "PRESENT."

YEAH, GOT IT.
...GRUMBLE...

COURTNEY HAD COME FROM A RELATIVELY MODEST NEIGHBORHOOD IN THE CITY, AND STOOD OUT AMONG HER PRIVILEGED CLASSMATES.

THAT FACT AND HER LAST NAME WERE ENOUGH TO GUARANTEE A ROUGH INTRODUCTION.
CRAZY OLD CRUMRIN'S GRAND-DAUGHTER...
WHAT ARE THOSE CLOTHES SHE'S WEARING?
I HEARD SHE COMES FROM THE GHETTO. SHE TALKS LIKE SHE'S FROM THE GHETTO.

ARE YOU REALLY RELATED TO OLD MAN CRUMRIN?
I HEARD HE'S SOME SORT OF LUNATIC OR AN EX-HIPPY OR SOMETHING.
YEAH, SO?

UH-OH...
LOOK. THE GREASE STAIN HAS A GIRLFRIEND.
THAT'S A GIRL? SHE LOOKS LIKE A Q-TIP.
Q-TIP! HA HA! THAT'S AWESOME!
THESE YOUR FRIENDS? IS THIS WHERE YOU ALL WAIT FOR THE SHORT BUS?

THE STAIN ISN'T REALLY A FRIEND, HE'S JUST MY FINANCIAL BACKER.
RIGHT, STAIN?

UH, RIGHT...
THAT'S RIGHT. HE AND SOME OTHER LAME-ASSES CONTRIBUTE TO OUR CAUSE.
SO, STAIN, WHAT'S MY QUARTERLY REPORT LOOK LIKE?

...HERE...
WHAT IS THIS, PERFORMANCE ART?
I THOUGHT YOU GUYS WERE ALL RICH 'R SOMETHIN'.
MY DAD'S RICH. I'M SURE YOU'VE HEARD OF HIM. AUGUSTUS OUDLER?
HE'S ON THE BOARD OF GOLDEN SACKS.

HE TOLD ME THAT I HAVE TO LEARN THE VALUE OF THE DOLLAR BY EARNING IT MYSELF, SO THAT'S WHAT I'M DOING.
WHAT'VE YOU GOT FOR ME, Q-TIP?

OKAY, I'M NOT GETTING THE JOKE.
HOW ABOUT THIS ONE? YOU LIKE APPLES?

HEY!!!
HOW DO YOU LIKE THEM APPLES!?!

COUGH!
SPUTTER!
TEN DOLLARS? WHAT THE HELL?
YOU BETTER HAVE MORE THAN THIS TOMORROW, Q-TIP.
OOF!
WUMP!
DON'T WORRY. THEY ONLY BEAT YOU UP THE FIRST FEW TIMES.
COUGH!
REMIND ME TO THANK THEM.

MUCH TO COURTNEY'S DISMAY, HER PARENTS SEEMED TO BE SETTLING IN NICELY...
OH, AND YOU SHOULD SEE THE HEALTH CLUB.

MASSAGES AVAILABLE TWENTY-FOUR HOURS A DAY.

MMMM...

RAN INTO JEB FINCH JOGGING THIS MORNING. YOU KNOW, THE D.A.

TERRIFIC GUY. RICH AS SIN.

HOW WAS YOUR FIRST DAY AT SCHOOL, HONEY?

...GRUMBLE...

HELLO?

THAT NIGHT, COURTNEY AGAIN FOUND HERSELF UNABLE TO SLEEP. SHE WANDERED THE STILL, QUIET HALLS, FILLED WITH A NAMELESS DREAD.
HELLO?

IS ANYBODY THERE?

THE LIGHT UNDER THE DOOR FELT WARM AND INVITING.
COURTNEY WAS AFRAID TO INCUR HER UNCLE'S WRATH, BUT HER DREAD OF THE LONELY HOUSE WAS MUCH MORE POWERFUL.
UNCLE ALOYSIUS?

FOR A MOMENT SHE FORGOT HER FEAR, AND STARED IN WONDER.

IT WAS LIKE A WIZARD'S DEN, FILLED WITH COUNTLESS STRANGE AND MAGICAL THINGS.

WOW...

THAT BOOK IS FOUR HUNDRED YEARS OLD. DO BE CAREFUL WITH IT.
IS THERE A REASON YOU'RE POKING AROUND IN MY PRIVATE CHAMBERS, YOUNG LADY?
I'M SORRY, SIR. I COULDN'T SLEEP.
TO COURTNEY'S WONDER AND RELIEF, THE OLD MAN'S EXPRESSION SOFTENED.
THIS HOUSE TAKES SOME GETTING USED TO. I'LL TAKE YOU BACK TO YOUR ROOM.
DON'T WORRY. NOTHING IN THIS HOUSE WILL HARM YOU.
NOW, HOW ABOUT THAT CUP OF COCOA?

TRY TO GET SOME SLEEP. IT WILL BE MORNING SOON.

THE NEXT DAY, COURTNEY FELT LIKE DEATH WARMED OVER. SHE WAS BEGINNING TO MAKE A DECIDEDLY POOR IMPRESSION ON HER TEACHER.

PROJECT:
calculate your net worth
MISS CRUMRIN, I MUST INSIST THAT YOU REMAIN AWAKE FOR MY CLASS.
I KNOW THAT I'M ASKING A LOT...

HEY, WAIT UP.
THE DAY HAD SEEMED INTERMINABLE. LITTLE DID SHE KNOW THAT THE WORST WAS YET TO COME.

WE SHOULD STICK *TOGETHER*, YOU KNOW?
YEAH. *TWO LOSERS* ARE BETTER THAN *ONE*.

HEY *LOOK*, IT'S AXEL AND THE *Q-TIP*. I HOPE YOU HAVE MORE *MONEY* TODAY, Q-TIP.
THEY'RE HERE *EVERYDAY*. MIGHT AS WELL GET IT *OVER* WITH.

C'MON, WE HAVEN'T GOT *ALL DAY*. WE HAVE TO HIT THE *MALL* AT *3:30*.
SCREW *THAT*. SHE TOOK MY *WHOLE WEEK'S ALLOWANCE* YESTERDAY.
YOU ONLY GET TEN DOLLARS A *WEEK*? WOW, THAT *SUCKS*.
THANKS FOR THE *SYMPATHY*.
WELL I AIN'T INTERESTED IN *THEIR* OPINION. *LATER*.
HEY, WHAT'RE YOU *DOING*?

NO ONE GOES INTO THE WOODS. THEY'RE HAUNTED.
WHAT?
IS IT EMBARRASSING?
BEING SO COMPLETELY PATHETIC?

HEY, WHERE DO YOU THINK YOU'RE GOING?

WAIT UP!
COURTNEY HEARD AXEL'S FOOTSTEPS FADE BEHIND HER AS SHE PLUNGED DEEPER AND DEEPER INTO THE TREES. HIS CALLS SLOWLY RECEDED.

BEFORE LONG SHE FOUND SHE NO LONGER KNEW WHICH WAY THE ROAD LAY.
JEEZ, COULD THIS TOWN POSSIBLY GET WEIRDER?

YOU BET IT COULD. AND COURTNEY WAS ABOUT TO FIND THAT OUT.
AXEL?

SORRY ABOUT THE LOSER THING. IT'S JUST...

HEY, I'M TALKING TO--

SLURP
SMACK
YOU...

ANOTHER ONE FOR DESSERT!
'OW LUVERLY!
Aaaaaaahhh!!!

WHEW

OH, THERE YOU ARE.
GOT YOUR CHECKBOOK READY?
...GRUMBLE...
weenci

WE DIDN'T RAISE OUR LITTLE GIRL TO GET INTO FIGHTS.

THIS IS A DECENT NEIGHBORHOOD. DO YOU WANT TO MAKE US LOOK BAD?

GO AWAY...

CRUNCH
CRUNCH

GO AWAY!

PLEASE...
>GNASH<

HHHSSSSSSSSSS

AAAAHHH!

Bang
Bang
Bang
UNCLE ALOYSIUS!?!

k klak

ANYONE HOME?

A Treatise on Goblins
On the Capture and Domestication of Goblins

A Bestiary of Night Things
Great and Small
A. Crumrin

AXEL WAS NEVER SEEN BY ANYONE IN HILLSBOROUGH AGAIN. I'M SORRY TO SAY THAT NO ONE MISSED HIM ALL THAT MUCH.
AFTER ALL, COURTNEY HAD HER OWN PROBLEMS TO DEAL WITH.
OH, WHAT A FINE JACKET Y'VE GOT THERE, MR. BUTTER-WORM.

WHY THANK'EE, MR. BUTTERWORM. IT COME OFF A PERFEK'LY TOOTHSOME LITTLE FELLER.
'OW DELIGHTFUL, MR. BUTTERWORM. AND WHERE BE THIS LITTLE FELLER NOW?

BUURRRRUPP!
I COULDN'T RIGHTLY TELL, MR. BUTTERWORM. P'RAPS ON HIS WAY TO ME LOWER INTESTYNES.
EHEM!

IT WAS A VERY HELPFUL CHAPTER THAT COURTNEY HAD FOUND.
REMEMBER ME?
MY DESSERT!!!

THERE WAS EVEN A SUBSECTION TITLED "ON CAPTURING AND BINDING OF GOBLINS".
COME BACK, ME DARLIN'! I'M STILL A MIGHT PECKISH!
BETTER MOVE FAST, FUZZY

DECENT OF YE TO PROVIDE ME SOME EXCERSIZE, LASS! I WERE BECOMIN' SLUGGISH!

DON'T YOU FRET, NOW. I'LL CATCH YE BY AND BY.

POOR SOFT-HEADED CHILD. EATEN'LL BE A BLESSIN' FOR HER.

SNIFF SNIFF
HA!

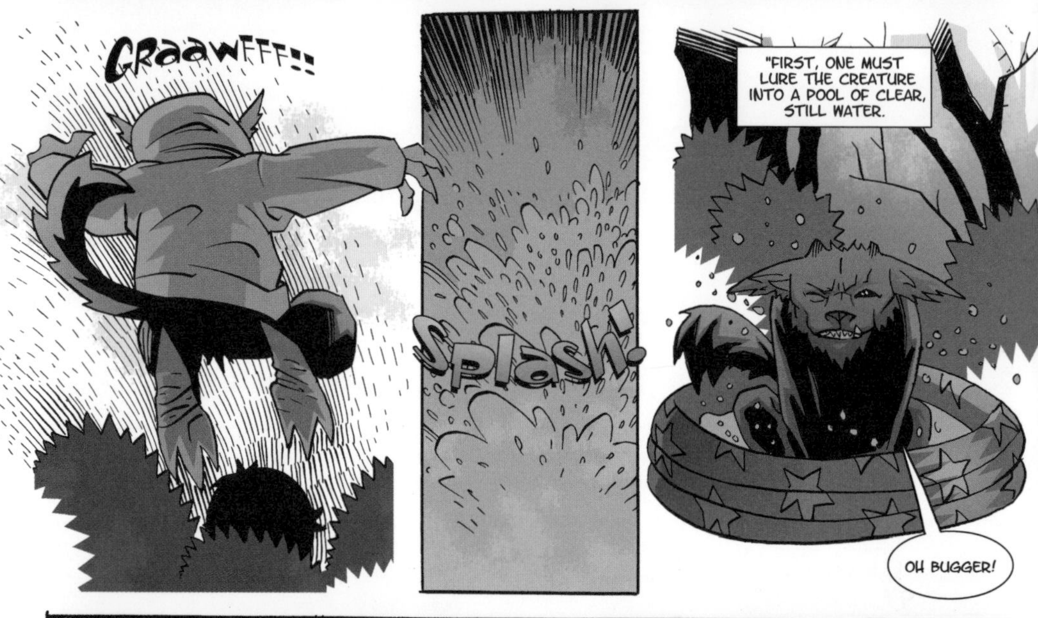
GRAAWFFF!!
SPLASH!
"FIRST, ONE MUST LURE THE CREATURE INTO A POOL OF CLEAR, STILL WATER.
OH BUGGER!

"DANDELION SEEDS WILL DISORIENT IT TEMPORARILY..."

"...UNTIL YOU CAN SECURELY BIND IT IN COLD IRON."
YE JUST THINK Y'RE ALL KINDSA CLEVER, DONT YE. MISSY?
I JUST DO MY HOMEWORK.

SEE YA.
YE LITTLE MONSTER! I'LL EAT YER FACE OFF!

LET ME OUT!

BUT THAT WASN'T THE END OF THE ESSAY.

"YOU MUST THEN WAIT FOR THREE DAYS AND THREE NIGHTS, AND RETURN AT DUSK ON THE FOURTH DAY."

Y-Y-YOU AG-GAIN...

COMFY?

I BROUGHT SOME FOOD. PB & J.
IT'S NOT WHAT YOU'RE USED TO, BUT...

CHOMP!
"IF THE GOBLIN THEN ACCEPTS FOOD FROM YOU...

"IT MUST GRANT YOU A BOON."
ALRIGHT, MISS SMARTY-PANTS. WHAD'YER WANT ME TO DO?

I'M GLAD YOU ASKED...

UNICORN
SO I SEE YOU'VE DECIDED TO STAY AND MAKE THE BEST OF IT.
alex web

OH, IT AIN'T SO BAD HERE.

ARE YOU MAKING NEW FRIENDS AT SCHOOL?

alex web
I'VE MET SOME PRETTY INTERESTING PEOPLE...

#1 KENSINGTON LANE.
THE OUDLER MANSION.

GOODNIGHT, ALICIA, MY DEAR. SWEET DREAMS.

G'NIGHT, DADDY.

WHO'S THERE!?!
DADDY?

Chapter Two

AS I'M SURE YOU CAN IMAGINE, COURTNEY HAD LITTLE SUCCESS IN MAKING FRIENDS AT HILLSBOROUGH JUNIOR HIGH.

SHE KNEW SHE WASN'T GOING TO BE MISS POPULARITY, BUT THUS FAR, A FULL THREE WEEKS AFTER HER ARRIVAL, SHE STILL HAD NO FRIENDS AT ALL...

AT LEAST, NONE WHO HADN'T BEEN EATEN.
SO I WAS THINKING ICE CREAM.

MM-HMM?
AND PERHAPS YOU AND MYSELF. PERHAPS SOME ICE CREAM SUNDAES.
MM-HMM?

I WAS THINKING TOMORROW AFTERNOON.

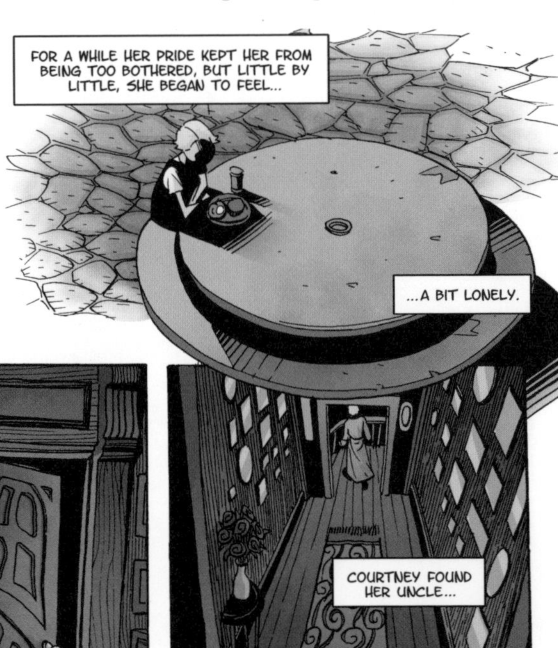
FOR A WHILE HER PRIDE KEPT HER FROM BEING TOO BOTHERED, BUT LITTLE BY LITTLE, SHE BEGAN TO FEEL...
...A BIT LONELY.

HER NEW HOME, HOWEVER, WAS ANOTHER MATTER ENTIRELY.
COURTNEY FOUND HER UNCLE...

...OR TO BE PRECISE, HER UNCLE'S UNUSUAL HOBBY...

...ENORMOUSLY INTRIGUING...

IF MORE OR LESS INCOMPREHENSIBLE.
BUT IT MUST MEAN SOMETHING, SHE TOLD HERSELF.
Chapter Six
The Beguiling Glamour
SURELY HER UNCLE WOULDN'T OWN STACKS OF BOOKS FILLED WITH TOTAL GIBBERISH.
...GLAMOW-ER.
OKEY-DOKEY.
HMMM...
The Eye of Horus must be invoked for magics of illusory or otherwise visually deceptive nature.
Ragwort
IT WAS DIFFICULT TO DECIPHER, BUT SHE THOUGHT SHE WAS BEGINNING TO GET THE IDEA.

SPRITES O' EARTH, I THEE COMMANDE, GRAUNT UPON ME EARTHLY SPLENDOUR...
THE HERBS REQUIRED WERE SURPRISINGLY COMMON, AND COURTNEY FOUND MANY OF THEM IN HER MOTHER'S HANDSOME BUT UNUSED SPICE RACK.
ENFOLDE ABOOT ME MANTLE FAIR...
AND BEAUTY'S POWER TAE ENGENDER.
...HMMM...
WELL, THAT WAS POINTLESS.

COURTNEY TRIED TO FEEL PHILOSOPHICAL ABOUT HER ISOLATION.
"THERE ARE WORSE THINGS THAN SOLITUDE," SHE THOUGHT TO HERSELF.

"I JUST CAN'T THINK OF ANY RIGHT NOW."

HEY, COURTNEY!
WHAT'S GOING ON?
HI, COURTNEY!

DO YOU WANNA HANG OUT THIS WEEKEND?
WHAT ARE YOU DOING AFTER SCHOOL?
WHAT DO YOU THINK OF THAT GARETH ROSSER? CUTE, HUH?

AND FOR THE REMAINDER OF THE DAY, COURTNEY CONTINUED TO BE THE CENTER OF ATTENTION.
Did your ancestors come over on the Mayflower?
AND WHY DID THE PATRIOTS ATTACK THE SHIPMENT?
COURTNEY?

OH, UM, BECAUSE PURITANS CAN'T HAVE CAFFEINE? SINFUL?

THAT'S A VERY... CREATIVE ANSWER. VERY GOOD, COURTNEY.
IT WAS ALSO BECAUSE IMPORT TAXES WERE EXTREMELY HIGH, AND THE COLONISTS FELT THEY WERE BEING EXPLOITED...

YEAH, GOT IT.

BUT I LIKE THE WAY YOUR MIND WORKS, YOUNG LADY.
KEEP IT UP.

BY LUNCHTIME, COURTNEY WAS BEGINNING TO SUSPECT SHE'D MADE A SERIOUS MISTAKE.
DO YOU WANT MY BANANA?
I HAVE CHOCOLATE CAKE.
DO YOU WANT MY SANDWICH?

SO THEN I SAY, "DON'T EVEN GO THERE." PRETTY COOL. HUH?
CAN YOU EVEN BELIEVE MEGAN WORE THAT DRESS? SHE LOOKS LIKE A SOFA.
AND THEN REG GOES, "WHATEVER!" AND I GO LIKE "DUH."

YES, GOD. I GET IT.
"BE CAREFUL WHAT YOU WISH FOR."
VERY CLEVER OBJECT LESSON.
SUSHI?

HE'D STOPPED HER MID-THOUGHT, AND LOOKING UP AT HIM, HER INSIDES TURNED TO ICEWATER.
WE HAVEN'T ACTUALLY HUNG OUT, HAVE WE?
UH...

COURTNEY CAREFULLY AVOIDED BOYS LIKE GARETH FOR EXACTLY THIS REASON. THEY MADE HER FEEL STRANGE IN WAYS THAT SHE DIDN'T QUITE UNDERSTAND.
BUT YOU DEFINITELY SEEM LIKE YOU'RE WORTH HANGING OUT WITH.
UH...
THANKS...

I WAS THINKING ICE CREAM. I KNOW THIS PLACE. IT'S PRETTY COOL.

SH--... SURE... COOL. I LIKE...
COOL.
MAYBE THIS SPELL CASTING WASN'T SUCH A BAD IDEA AFTER ALL.

GREAT.
SEE YOU AFTER SCHOOL.

OKAY.

Smedley Hoohah Ice Cream Parlor
GOOD ICE CREAM.
IT'S OKAY. THE BEST ICE CREAM COMES FROM A PLACE IN THE CITY.
EVER BEEN?
YEAH, I USED TO-
MY DAD WON'T LET ME GO EITHER. HE HAS HIS P.A. DRIVE OUT THERE AND PICK IT UP.
THAT MUST BE...
HE'S THE CEO OF THIS REALLY BIG SOFTWARE COMPANY.
HE WAS BROUGHT IN TO MAKE THE COMPANY SALEABLE, AND THEN WHEN THEY GET SOLD HE'LL GET A HUGE BONUS.
THAT'S WHAT HE DOES.
GREAT.
HE PROMISED ME A MERCURY MOUNTAINEER FOR MY SIXTEENTH BIRTHDAY. THAT'S A REALLY COOL SUV.
UH-HUH...

HE THINKS HE'S SO COOL.
SHE'S TOTALLY BORED. LOOK.
I'M COOLER THAN HE IS.
LET'S GO IN THERE.

YOUR PARENTS WILL BE EXCITED THAT YOU'RE FRIENDS WITH ME.
THEY'VE BEEN WANTING TO MEET MY DAD.
HEY, ROSSER!

YOU'VE HAD YOUR CHANCE. LET ME SHOW YOU HOW IT'S DONE.
HEY, COURTNEY. IS THIS GUY BOTHERING YOU?

BACK OFF, REG.
YOU'RE TOO SLOW, GUY.

YOU BETTER ALL CLEAR OFF IF YOU KNOW WHAT'S GOOD FOR YOU!
OH YEAH?

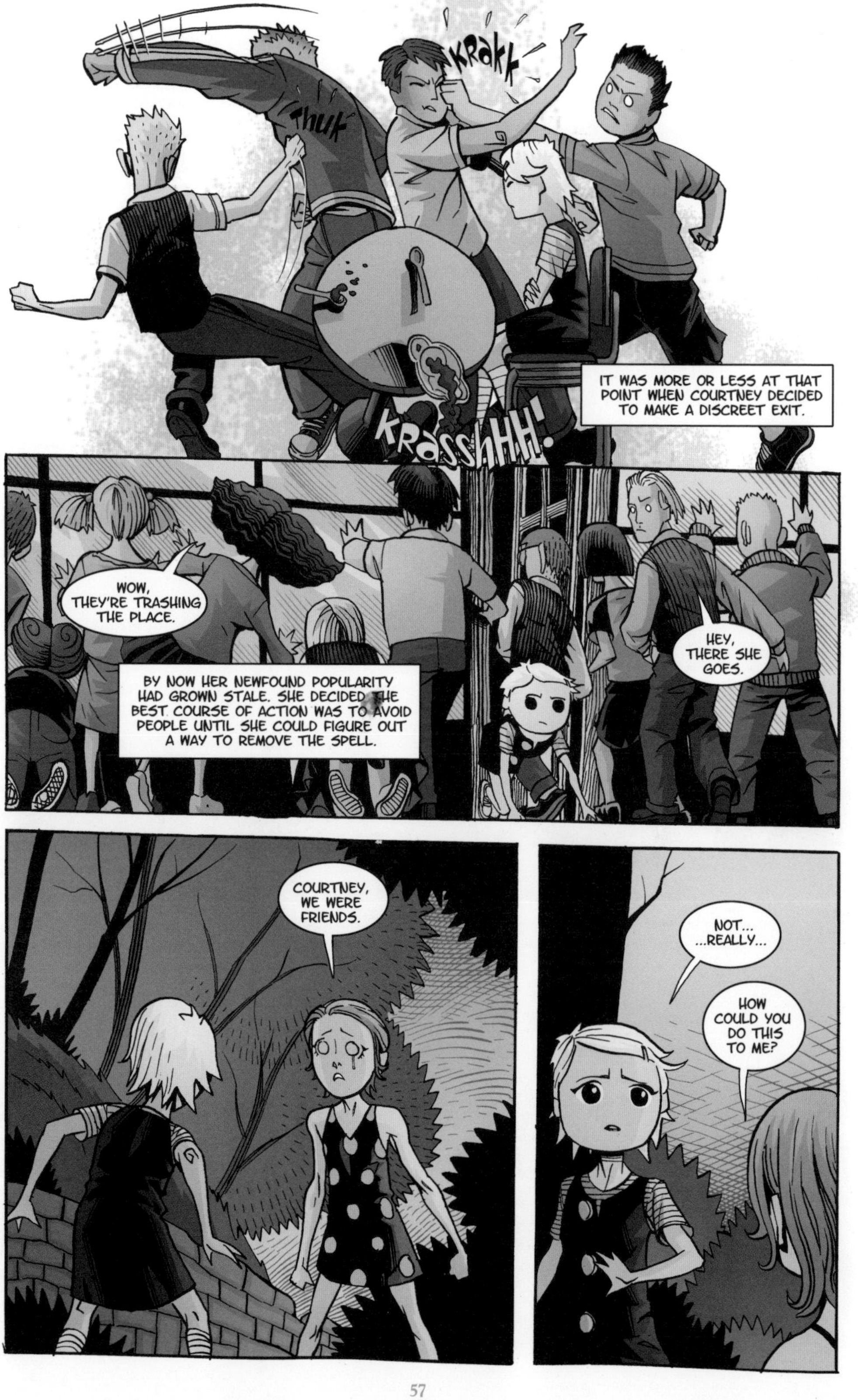

KRAKK

THUK

KRASSHHH!

IT WAS MORE OR LESS AT THAT POINT WHEN COURTNEY DECIDED TO MAKE A DISCREET EXIT.

WOW, THEY'RE TRASHING THE PLACE.

BY NOW HER NEWFOUND POPULARITY HAD GROWN STALE. SHE DECIDED THE BEST COURSE OF ACTION WAS TO AVOID PEOPLE UNTIL SHE COULD FIGURE OUT A WAY TO REMOVE THE SPELL.

HEY, THERE SHE GOES.

COURTNEY, WE WERE FRIENDS.

NOT... ...REALLY...
HOW COULD YOU DO THIS TO ME?

GARETH WAS GOING TO GO OUT WITH ME.
WE WERE GOING TO HAVE ICE CREAM.
OH, THAT'S RIGHT. I FORGOT...

HOW DARE YOU? YOU WERE MY BEST FRIEND! YOU STABBED ME IN THE HEART!!! AM I SOME KIND OF JOKE TO YOU?
BEST FRIEND? SINCE RECESS?

I HATE YOU!!!
I HATE YOU!!!
HEY!!!

YOU CAN'T TALK TO COURTNEY LIKE THAT.
YEAH! WHO DO YOU THINK YOU ARE?

THINGS WEREN'T LOOKING GOOD FOR CATHY. COURTNEY OPTED NOT TO STAY AND WATCH.
LEAVE ME ALONE!!!

AT HOME, THINGS WERE JUST AS UNSETTLING. COURTNEY WAS DEEPLY DISTURBED TO REALIZE THAT HER PARENTS' ADORATION WAS EVEN LESS PLEASANT THAN THEIR INDIFFERENCE.

HOW'S MY LITTLE ANGEL TODAY?

I HEARD YOU'VE BEEN SPENDING TIME WITH GARETH ROSSER'S KID. THAT'S MY GIRL.

YOU ACTUALLY LOOK NICE TODAY. ARE YOU DOING SOMETHING WITH YOUR HAIR FOR A CHANGE?

BY CONTRAST, UNCLE ALOYSIUS SEEMED THE SAME AS EVER.

MAYBE NOT QUITE THE SAME.

PERHAPS THIS WAS HIS WAY OF EXPRESSING INTEREST.
Bong Bung

COULD TONIGHT POSSIBLY GET ANY MORE UNCOMFORTABLE?

ASK A SILLY QUESTION...
YEAH, SO WE NEED TO TALK.

SURE. WE'LL DO LUNCH SOMETIME.
KaKlak

BONG BUNG
BONG BUNG
BONG BUNG
BONG BUNG
BONG BUNG
BONG BUNG

FOR CRYIN' OUT LOUD!
I'M IN LOVE WITH YOU.

OW!!!
KRUNCH

I CAN STAND HERE RINGING THE DOORBELL ALL NIGHT.
WHO IS IT, SWEETHEART?
IS IT HOOLIGANS?
IS IT GARETH JUNIOR?

FINE! OUTSIDE.
WE'LL TALK OUTSIDE.

DOESN'T IT MEAN ANYTHING TO YOU?
I LOVE YOU. I! ME!
GARETH-
IT'S WEIRD. YOU'RE SO WRONG FOR ME.
YOU'RE SUCH A LOSER.
THANKS.

YOU'RE LIKE... SO INTENSE. YOU KNOW?
BUT I'VE BEEN OBSESSED WITH YOU SINCE THE FIRST DAY YOU APPEARED.
UM...

I CAN TOTALLY TELL YOU'RE A DEEP THINKER.
AND AN ARTIST.
AM I?

YOU'RE A BEAUTIFUL PERSON, COURTNEY. INSIDE.
A TENDER HEART. YOU'RE A SENSITIVE SOUL, YOU KNOW?

OKAY, THAT'S IT. JUST SHUT UP.
BUT--

SHUT UP, GARETH. GO HOME.
I'LL SEE YOU TOMORROW, AND I PROMISE YOU'LL FEEL TOTALLY DIFFERENT.
WHAT?
YOU'LL GO BACK TO IGNORING ME, LIKE NATURE INTENDED.
I HOPE.
WHAT ARE YOU SAYING? YOU'RE REJECTING ME!!!
WHO DO YOU THINK YOU ARE!?!
YOU SHOULD BE THANKFUL THAT I EVEN TALK TO YOU!
OW!!! LEGGO!!!
I LOVE YOU, YOU HEAR ME!?!
MMMPH!!!

GAAHH!!!

OW!!!
YOU FREAK!!!

COURTNEY! WAIT!

I'M SORRY, ALRIGHT!?!
COME BACK!

HEY, DID YOU JUST SEE A GIRL RUN PAST?
AS A MATTER O' FACT, LAD...

I DID!

AAAAAAAHHHHH!!!

PHEW!

WE NEED TO HAVE A LITTLE CHAT, YOUNG LADY.

I FOUND THESE IN YOUR ROOM.
I'M VERY SORRY, SIR.
I UNDERSTAND YOUR CURIOSITY.

AND I IMAGINE YOU'VE NOTICED HOW DANGEROUS SUCH POWER CAN BE.

OH YEAH.
YOU'RE LUCKY. YOU SAW ONLY THE TIP OF THE ICEBERG.

IT COULD HAVE BEEN MUCH WORSE.
IT WAS GETTING PRETTY BAD FOR A WHILE.

YOU DID DRAW ATTENTION TO YOURSELF, SOMETHING AN INTELLIGENT WITCH TRIES TO AVOID.
WITCH?

I'M TELLING YOU THIS IN CONFIDENCE, COURTNEY.
DO I LOOK INFIRM?
HUH? NO, NOT REALLY.
COURTNEY, IF I REALLY NEEDED LOOKING AFTER, THE LAST PEOPLE I WOULD ASK WOULD BE MY IDIOT GRANDNEPHEW AND HIS WIFE.
I'M NOT GETTING IT.

THEY GATHERED INGREDIENTS AND ALOYSIUS TAUGHT COURTNEY THE PROPER INCANTATION, PATIENTLY CORRECTING HER WHEN SHE MISPRONOUNCED THE WORDS.
SINCE COURTNEY HAD CAST THE SPELL TWICE, SHE NEEDED TO CAST THE COUNTER-SPELL A SECOND TIME AS WELL.
SHADOWS LO' BENEATH THE MOON, ATTEND THIS UNCOUTH SOUL, STRIP AWAY ILL-GOTTEN GRACE, AND TRUTH TAKE ITS TOLL.

BETTER DO *ONE MORE* TO MAKE SURE.
I *WOULDN'T.*

TO CAST A *COUNTER-SPELL* WHERE THERE'S NO *SPELL* WOULD HAVE THE *OPPOSITE EFFECT.*

OH, *REALLY?*

AAAHH...

SO YEAH, COURTNEY. I WAS THINKING...
YOU WEREN'T GOING TO MENTION... LAST NIGHT... OR... ANYTHING THAT HAPPENED... TO ANYONE. WERE YOU?
HADN'T REALLY THOUGHT ABOUT IT.
WELL IT'S JUST THAT, YOU KNOW, IT WOULD PROBABLY BE BETTER IF YOU DIDN'T MENTION IT.
IT MIGHT MAKE... US BOTH... ...LOOK BAD.
MOSTLY YOU. I'M JUST THINKING OF YOUR REPUTATION.
GEE. THANKS.

STRIP AWAY
ILL-GOTTEN GRACE,
AND TRUTH TAKE
ITS TOLL.

COME
AGAIN?
OH,
NOTHING.

BOY,
YOU ARE
WEIRD.

SO, CATHY.
WHERE DO YOU
WANT ME TO SIGN
THAT CAST?

GO
CLIMB A ROPE,
GARETH.

Chapter Three

THE WHOLE MESS ESSENTIALLY BEGAN OVER DRINKS AT THE HILLSBOROUGH MIDDLE SCHOOL PARENTS' SOCIAL.
HILLSBOROUGH MIDDLE SCHOOL

THIS WAS A CAREFULLY ORCHESTRATED MANEUVER OF THE SORT THAT MRS. CRUMRIN WAS WELL PRACTICED.

WATCH CLOSELY...

EVELYN DEAR...

I'VE HEARD YOU'VE HAD TROUBLE FINDING ADEQUATE CHILDCARE.

WHAT A DISASTER.

YOU'D THINK MAYOR TATE WOULD HAVE A BETTER BEHAVED DAUGHTER.

SHE SEEMED POLITE ENOUGH AT FIRST.

BUT HONESTLY! WHO KNEW THAT TEENAGERS COULD CAUSE SUCH DAMAGE?

THEY'D TURNED THE HOUSE INTO A DISCO.
THERE WERE SIX OR SEVEN OF THEM, PLAYING THAT LOUD THUMPY MUSIC. THE CARPET IS BEYOND HELP.
OH HONEY...
ADD TO THAT SIX BOTTLES OF ROERDERER. CAN YOU IMAGINE?
HOW AWFUL.
AND SEVERAL HUNDRED DOLLARS IN LONG DISTANCE BILLS TO SOME YOUTH HOSTEL IN AMSTERDAM.

YOU POOR-
OH! WHAT A SHAME.

ISN'T ROERDERER A THOUSAND DOLLARS A BOTTLE?

YOU POOR DEAR.
YOU KNOW, IF YOU'RE STILL IN THE MARKET FOR A SITTER...
SUBTLE, ISN'T SHE?

JEBEDIAH FINCH, IN ADDITION TO BEING THE DISTRICT ATTORNEY FOR THE WHOLE COUNTY, CAME FROM OLD MONEY.
HE AND HIS WIFE WERE SOME OF THE MOST RESPECTED MEMBERS OF THE COMMUNITY...

AND ANY FRIENDS OF THEIRS WERE, BY PROXY, ALSO HIGHLY RESPECTABLE.
ISN'T SHE A LITTLE YOUNG?
MAYBE, BUT LOOK AT IT THIS WAY.
OF ALL THE GIRLS IN THE NEIGHBORHOOD, COURTNEY CRUMRIN IS THE LEAST LIKELY TO THROW A WILD PARTY.

HEH HEH, OR RUN UP PHONE BILLS.
AND I LOCKED THE LIQUOR CABINET, JUST IN CASE.
IT'S FUNNY. WHEN I WAS A KID, WE ALL LIVED IN MORTAL TERROR OF THE CRUMRIN HOUSE.
I WOULD NEVER HAVE IMAGINED THAT THE OCCUPANTS WOULD BE SO...
I DON'T KNOW...
I THINK THE WORD YOU'RE LOOKING FOR IS "BANAL."
HEH...
THEY DON'T EXACTLY RADIATE MYSTERY AND TERROR, DO THEY?

GREAT. THANKS. WELL, THAT'S IT, I THINK. LET'S GET GOING, DEAR.
COURTNEY, NOW DON'T LET BOO INTO THE ROOM.

I DON'T WANT HIM FALLING ASLEEP ON ROGER'S LITTLE HEAD AGAIN.

YOU HEAR THAT, HONEY?
SO ANYWAY EVELYN, WHO DO WE HAVE TO KILL TO GET INVITED TO MAYOR TATE'S FUNDRAISER NEXT MONTH?

SWEETY, DON'T BE WEIRD.
...GRUMBLE...

THIS IS MORE OR LESS HOW COURTNEY ENDED UP BABY-SITTING THE FINCHES' NEWBORN.
COURTNEY DIDN'T LIKE BABIES AT THE BEST OF TIMES. AS FAR AS SHE WAS CONCERNED, ANYTHING THAT EXISTED SOLELY TO EMIT DROOL, VOMIT, GHASTLY ODORS, AND LOUD, ANNOYING SCREAMS WAS MORE TROUBLE THAN IT WAS WORTH.
NEEDLESS TO SAY, HER PARENTS HADN'T BOTHERED TO CONSULT HER IN THE MATTER.
THE ONLY UPSIDE WAS THE FINCHES' SATELLITE DISH.
YOU'RE WATCHING THE FAMILY LEARNING CHANNEL.
AND NOW, ANGRY TICKS FIRE OUT OF MY NIPPLES.

WHAT THE... ?

BRRR
ONE CREEPY BABY...
BET HE GROWS UP TO BE A DIVORCE ATTORNEY.

ALL RIGHT!
WHAT THE HECK IS GOING ON IN HERE?

I KNOW I HEARD SOMETHING...
WHAT'S THE DEAL?
bwah?

WHAT'VE YOU GOT THERE?

gurgle

...HUH...

NICE. I SUPPOSE I'LL GET BLAMED FOR THIS.

NOW HOW'D-

NOW WHAT!?!

WHAT HAVE YOU GOT NOW?

YOU GOTTA BE KIDDING...
Burrrrupp*

SOMETHING SERIOUSLY WRONG WITH THAT KID.

PROBABLY ALREADY HAVE HIM ON PROZAC.
...GRUMBLE...

UMM... CAN I HELP YOU?

RRRRaaawww!!!!

THAT USUALLY SCARES THE BEJEEZUS OUT OF LITTLE GIRLS.
I'M GONNA GO OUT ON A LIMB AND GUESS YOU'RE NOT ACTUALLY A BABY.
WHAT TIPPED YOU OFF, TOOTS?
FOR ONE THING, YOU SMELL EVEN WORSE THAN A HUMAN INFANT.
WHISKEY ALWAYS GIVES ME THE WIND...

WHERE'S THE REAL BABY!?!

HEY!!!
WHERE DO YOU THINK YOU'RE GOING WITH THAT BABY!?!

DAMMIT!!!

TOLD YOU.
WHERE ARE THEY TAKING HIM!?!

THE MARKET, OF COURSE.
WHAT!?!
DON'T WORRY. THEY RARELY EVER GET EATEN ANYMORE. TOO EXPENSIVE.
HE'LL GO TO A GOOD HOME, I'M SURE.

YOU LITTLE--
CAREFUL, GIRLY. YOU'LL GET YOURSELF IN A WHOLE MESS OF TROUBLE.
SPROING!

KRASH
THUNK
COME BACK HERE!!!
STOP THAT.
OH, DEAR ME. WHAT WILL THE FINCHES SAY WHEN THEY SEE THE MESS YOU'VE MADE?

I'M GONNA KILL YOU!!!
TEMPER TEMPER, YOUNG LADY.

HEE HEE HEE...

WHOOPS!
KRAASHHH

OH, THIS IS JUST GONNA BE WAY TOO MUCH FUN...

WHOOPS...
I DO KNOW HOW TO PLAY HIDE AND SEEK, YA KNOW.

COMFY?
BLEARGH
LET'S TALK ABOUT THAT BABY, SHALL WE?
I CAN'T. I'M SWORN TO SECRECY.

YOU SURE?
TO TALK OF THESE THINGS WITH MORTALS IS FORBIDDEN.

YAAAAAAAHHHH!!!
FINE.

FEEL LIKE TALKING NOW?
IT'S IN THE CHANGELING UNION BYLAWS.
I'LL LOSE MY PENSION!

HAVE IT YOUR WAY.
GAAAAAAAAHHHH!!!

OOOF, I'M GONNA BARF!
BE MY GUEST. WE'RE GONNA BE SPINNING ALL NIGHT.
ENOUGH!

WHO SAID THAT!?!
WHO'S THERE?

I'LL TELL YOU WHERE THEY TOOK THE CHILD, IF THAT'S WHAT IT TAKES TO GET SOME PEACE IN THIS HOUSE.

...HUH?

GONNA BE ONE OF THOSE NIGHTS, I GUESS.
SO, BOO, YOU WERE FILLING ME IN ON THIS MUNCHKIN'S LITTLE DEAL?
IT'S AN ANCIENT PRACTICE. A CHANGELING TAKES THE PLACE OF THE STOLEN CHILD.
USUALLY THE PARENTS ARE NEVER THE WISER.
GREAT. GIVE AWAY THE WHOLE SHOW, WHY DON'T YOU.

HAH!!!

OH, IT'S YOU.

HELLO, BUTTERWORM. WE WERE JUST TAKING A STROLL DOWN TO GOBLIN TOWN.

BUT IT'S FORBIDDEN FOR...
OKAY. BEEN NICE KNOWIN' YE.
THAT'S WHAT WE TOLD HER.
YE LITTLE BRAT.
GEE, THANKS.

SO WHAT DO THE NIGHT THINGS WANT WITH YUPPIE-LARVAE ANYWAY?
I COULDN'T BEGIN TO IMAGINE. I CERTAINLY HAVE NO USE FOR THEM.

THEY FETCH A GOOD PRICE ON THE DARK MARKET. THE ELDER ONES RAISE THEM AS THEIR OWN.

NICE. SO, BOO, WHAT'S YOUR STORY, ANYWAY?
NO STORY, MADAM. JUST A CAT.
JUST YOUR GARDEN VARIETY TALKING HOUSE CAT. GOTCHA.

CONSIDERING YOUR LINEAGE, MISS CRUMRIN, I'M SURPRISED HOW LITTLE YOU KNOW OF THE WORLD.
UH HUH.

FOR A MOMENT, COURTNEY GAZED, TRANSFIXED, INTO THE VELVET DARKNESS OF THE TUNNEL. SHE SUSPECTED THAT SHE WAS ABOUT TO BITE OFF MORE THAN SHE COULD CHEW.

YET, SHE HAD LITTLE CHOICE BUT TO PRESS ON, IN THE HOPES THAT HER WITS AND HER LUCK WOULDN'T FAIL HER.

Goblin Town

REMEMBER, CHILD. TAKE NO FOOD NOR DRINK ONCE YOU PASS WITHIN.

YOU TREAD ON DANGEROUS GROUND HERE.

no food or drinks beyond this point

WELL, GOOD LUCK, KIDDO. I'LL JUST BE ON MY WAY.

NOT SO FAST, SHORTY.

YOU'RE GONNA TAKE ME RIGHT TO HIM.
BUT...
OR WE CAN SEE WHAT HAPPENS WHEN WE PUT THE BABY IN THE MICROWAVE.
...GRUMBLE...
THAT'S THE SPIRIT.

DESPITE HER BRAVADO, COURTNEY WAS FIGHTING OFF A BRIEF IMPULSE TO RUN SCREAMING INTO THE NIGHT.
TAKING A DEEP BREATH, SHE RESOLVED HERSELF TO THE TASK. "AFTER ALL," SHE THOUGHT TO HERSELF, "THIS CAN'T BE AS BAD AS CHANGING DIAPERS..."
WHO GOES THERE?

WE SMELL A MORTAL MAIDEN.
CHANGELING, ARE THE PATHS OF THE NIGHT FOR MORTAL FEET?
WHY DID YOU BRING THIS CHILD?
UH... NO, NO, SHE'S A... WOOD NYMPH, SEE?
IS SHE?

THAT'S RIGHT. I LOST MY WINGS IN A FREAK ACCIDENT, OKAY?
BACK OFF!

VERY CONVINCING.
SHUT UP!

SOON COURTNEY COULD NO LONGER RECALL WHICH WAY THEY HAD COME.
SHE BEGAN TO SUSPECT THE CHANGELING WAS LEADING HER ASTRAY.
THIS BETTER NOT TAKE MUCH LONGER, PIPSQUEAK.
WE'RE ALMOST THERE.
WHERE?
THE DARK MARKET.
AS HE SPOKE, THE TUNNEL OPENED OUT, AND COURTNEY FOUND HERSELF BREATHLESS, LOOKING UPON A CITY OF NIGHT THINGS.
SHE SAW STRANGE OUTLANDISH CREATURES EVERYWHERE, SHOUTING AND LAUGHING IN UNEARTHLY VOICES.
OH BOY.

THE SCENT OF MAGICAL FRUIT AND SPICES ASSAILED HER NOSTRILS, AND THE BRILLIANT LANTERNS DAZZLED HER EYES. SHE BEGAN TO GROW DIZZY.
WOW, THIS PLACE IS...
...KINDA COOL.
KEEP YOUR HEAD STRAIGHT, GIRL.
WHICH WAY?
THERE, THE SLAVE AUCTIONS.

SUDDENLY COURTNEY FOUND HERSELF CAUGHT IN A CROWD OF OTHERWORLDLY MONSTERS, ALL PUSHING AND SHOVING UP AGAINST HER.
SWEET MEATS, M'LADY?
FAERY APPLES, FRESH FROM TIR NAN OG.
SYLVAN HONEY WINE. FROM THE NECTAR OF MALLORN BLOSSOMS.
NO, PLEASE!

AND HER LADYSHIP TAKES IT FOR TWENTY SOVEREIGNS.

NEXT WE HAVE A MORTAL CHILD, FINE STOCK AND FULL OF INNOCENCE.
LET'S START THE BIDDING AT ONE HUNDRED SOVEREIGNS. WHO WILL BEGIN?

HEY, THAT'S HIM!
ONE, PLEASE.

I HAVE ONE HUNDRED FROM HIS FEROCIOUS LORDSHIP. DO I HEAR ONE TWENTY?

WE HAVE AN EAGER BUYER, FOLKS!
I'M SORRY, YOUNG LADY, YOU'LL HAVE TO MAKE A BID.

THAT'S MY BABY!!!
I CAN'T BELIEVE I JUST SAID THAT.

INDEED IT IS, FOR A MERE ONE HUNDRED TWENTY SOVEREIGNS.

ALE?
FRESH BREAD?
EXOTIC SPICES?

NO!!!

COUGH COUGH COUGH...
CHOKE

HERE, DRINK THIS.
COUGH
THANKS.

NO PROBLEM.

YOU LITTLE...

I WARNED YOU, CHILD.

...STUPID CAT...
AND THEN COURTNEY REMEMBERED NO MORE.

WHEN SHE CAME TO HERSELF AGAIN, SHE DISCOVERED THAT HER PREDICAMENT HAD GONE FROM BAD...

TO WORSE.
UH OH.
AND NOW, LADIES AND GENTLECREATURES, A MORTAL MAIDEN, OF THE SORT QUEEN TITANIA WAS SO FOND.
WE'LL START THE BIDDING AT FIFTY.

COURTNEY STARED OUT FROM HER CAGE AT THE GATHERED BIDDERS. THEY WERE GRIM AND MYSTERIOUS, AND SHE UNHAPPILY CONTEMPLATED WHAT THEY MIGHT HAVE IN MIND FOR HER.

NO ONE BIDS FIFTY? HOW ABOUT FORTY? FORTY SOVEREIGNS FOR THE MAIDEN.

THEN SHE SAW BOO AGAIN.

IF NO ONE TAKES HER, WE'LL BE FORCED TO THROW HER INTO THE MARL PIT FOR OLD RAWHEAD AND BLOODY BONES.

FORTY SOVEREIGNS SAVE THIS POOR WRETCH FROM A GHASTLY FATE.
SON OF A...

DO I HEAR FORTY?
SUDDENLY, EVERYTHING BECAME CLEAR. THE NEFARIOUS ANIMAL HAD TRICKED COURTNEY, LURING HER DOWN INTO GOBLIN TOWN FOR SOME DREAD PURPOSE.

FORTY SOVEREIGNS. I HAVE FORTY, DO I HEAR FIFTY?

FIFTY.
I HAVE FIFTY, DO I HEAR SIXTY?

SIXTY, HIS LORDSHIP BIDS SIXTY.
SEVENTY, THE LADY BIDS SEVENTY.
COURTNEY WANTED TO SCREAM, SHOUT INSULTS AT THE AUCTIONEER, ANYTHING TO STOP WHAT WAS HAPPENING. BUT HER SHOCK AND DISORIENTATION RENDERED HER QUITE INCAPABLE OF ACTION.

ALL SHE COULD DO WAS WATCH IN MUTE HORROR AS HER FATE WAS DECIDED BY LIVING NIGHTMARES.
EIGHTY FROM HIS LORDSHIP. NINETY FROM HER DREADFULNESS. DO I HEAR ONE HUNDRED?
NINETY. GOING ONCE. TWICE.

ONE HUNDRED. THANK YOU, SIR.

YOU SET ME UP, DIDN'T YOU?
I DID WARN YOU, MADAM.
GOBLIN TOWN IS NO PLACE FOR MORTALS.

WHAT I GET FOR TRUSTING A TALKING CAT.
PERHAPS...

AS THEY PULLED AWAY AND DROVE OFF INTO THE DARK TUNNELS, THE FULL HORROR OF HER SITUATION SWEPT OVER COURTNEY.
IT'S JUST... NOT FAIR.

AFTER A TIME, THE CARRIAGE SLOWED TO A HALT, AND ITS SOLE OCCUPANT STEPPED OUT.
OH CRAP.

AS COURTNEY'S CAPTOR APPROACHED, HER TERROR BECAME WILD PANIC. SHE REALIZED NOW THAT NOTHING SHORT OF A MIRACLE COULD SAVE HER.
UNCLE A, WHERE ARE YOU?
I NEED SOME HELP HERE.

I'M RIGHT HERE, COURTNEY.
YOU'RE NOT ESPECIALLY SHARP TODAY, ARE YOU?

BUT... HOW DID YOU...?
YOUR LITTLE FRIEND HERE TIPPED ME OFF.

AND LUCKY FOR YOU THAT HE DID.
I WOULD NEVER HAVE IMAGINED A CLEVER GIRL LIKE YOU COULD GET HERSELF INTO SUCH AN ABSURD PREDICAMENT.
AND WHAT WAS I SUPPOSED TO DO?
EXPLAIN TO MRS. FINCH THAT HER BABY'S BEEN KIDNAPPED AND REPLACED BY AN EVIL MUPPET?

EVELYN FINCH? SHE'D NEVER NOTICE.

BUT THE BABY! HE'S BEEN SOLD TO THAT FREAKY LIZARD LADY.

I'M TOUCHED BY YOUR CONCERN. BUT THESE THINGS HAPPEN, COURTNEY.

I WOULDN'T TROUBLE ABOUT IT IF I WERE YOU.
LITTLE ROGER WAS LONG GONE, BUT THE CHANGELING STILL HAD A JOB TO DO.

THEY FOUND HIM AT A LOCAL ALEHOUSE, GAMBLING AWAY THE MONEY HE'D MADE SELLING COURTNEY.
WOO HOO! BOYS, LOOKS LIKE MY LUCK IS FINALLY CHANGING....
EHEM!

REMEMBER ME?
OH BUGGER!

ULTIMATELY THEY PERSUADED HIM TO RETURN TO HIS DUTIES.
IT'S JUST NOT FAIR.

THANKS, UNCLE A.
BE MORE CAREFUL NEXT TIME. I WON'T ALWAYS BE THERE TO RESCUE YOU.
AND AFTER A FEW HELPFUL SPELLS THAT DEALT WITH THE REFORMING OF DISJOINED MATTER, HE DEPARTED.

OH, HEY. DID YOU CRAZY KIDS HAVE FUN TONIGHT?

WE SURE DID. SO COULD YOU COME BACK AGAIN NEXT WEEK?
FIFTY DOLLARS A NIGHT...

NO PROBLEM.

Chapter Four

I STILL CAN'T BELIEVE THEY CANCELLED ALLIE MCSHPEAL.
HEY, GUYS, WHAT'S WITH THE BIG CAR OUT THERE?
UNCLE ALOYSIUS IS GOING OUT OF TOWN.

HOW COME?
HE'S GOING TO ONE OF THOSE SWISS CLINICS.

MAYBE THAT ONE THAT KEITH RICHARDS GOES TO.
OH, I KNOW. I'M SO JEALOUS.

WHAT'S WRONG WITH HIM?! IS HE OKAY?
NOW, HONEY, YOU KNOW THAT HE'S AWFULLY OLD, AND HIS HEALTH IS FRAGILE.

NONSENSE. I'M JUST OFF TO TAKE CARE OF SOME BUSINESS.

OH... OKAY.

IN THE MEANTIME, YOU STAY OUT OF TROUBLE.

YEAH, WHATEVER.

I MEAN IT. NO ADVENTURES. NO LITTLE SCHEMES.

I DON'T WANT TO COME HOME AND FIND YOU'VE SOLD YOUR PARENTS INTO FAERY SERVITUDE.

YEAH, I GOT IT.

NO BIGGY, UNCLE A. I GOT MOM AND DAD TO KEEP ME ENTERTAINED.

AND SO THE DAYS WENT BY. BUT COURTNEY FOUND HERSELF MISSING THE STRANGE OLD MAN MUCH MORE THAN SHE EXPECTED.

SHE TRIED TO FALL BACK ON HER OLD HABITS.

SPOKEN TO MRS. FINCH LATELY?

SAW HER AT THE GROCERY STORE, BUT I COULDN'T CATCH UP.

FOR A WOMAN PUSHING A SHOPPING CART FILLED WITH WINE, SHE SURE CAN MOVE FAST.

KNOW WHAT YOU MEAN. JEB'S THE SAME WAY.
I JUST CAN'T KEEP UP WITH HIM JOGGING. THEY REALLY PUSH THEMSELVES.
IT'S SO INSPIRING. SUCH GREAT PEOPLE.
BUT WATCHING HER PARENTS DIDN'T PROVIDE AS MUCH DIVERSION AS IT ONCE HAD.

NOT HAVING REAL FRIENDS WAS SOMETHING THAT COURTNEY HAD LEARNED TO LIVE WITH. BUT IT HAD ITS SHORTCOMINGS.
SO NOW IT'S YOUR TURN. TAKE THE DICE.
MUH!

TAKE 'EM.

MUH!

...GRUMBLE...
CRUNCH
CRUNCH
CRUNCH

FORGET IT.

YOU TOO, HANDSOME. OUT!

SLAMM!
AND SHE BEGAN TO WONDER WHY SHE HAD SO MUCH TROUBLE FINDING ANYBODY WORTH SPENDING TIME WITH.

Hillsborough Wine Merchant
Drive in Video
COURTNEY'S DESPONDENCY SLOWLY GREW. ALL AROUND HER, THE OTHER CHILDREN HAPPILY BABBLED AWAY...

CHECK IT OUT. THE LATEST.
DUDE!
AWESOME.
I WANT ONE.

Tight-wad Fitness
open 24hrs
...AND ADULTS OCCUPIED THEMSELVES WITH INEXPLICABLE ACTIVITIES.
AND ONE...
TWO...
THREE...
FOUR...

COURTNEY WAS A PRACTICAL GIRL, AND IT BEGAN TO OCCUR TO HER THAT PERHAPS SHE WAS MISSING SOMETHING ABOUT THE WORLD. SOMETHING IMPORTANT.
AND BREATHE...
TWO...
THREE...
FOUR...

AFTER ALL, WHAT WAS MORE LIKELY? THAT THE WORLD WAS FILLED WITH COMPLETE DOOFUSES?
OR THAT THERE MIGHT BE SOMETHING WRONG WITH HER?

ONE MORNING, COURTNEY AWOKE AND FELT AS THOUGH HER DESPONDENCY HAD BECOME A PHYSICAL AILMENT.
BREAKFAST, COURTNEY!
MMMMPH.

DON'T FEEL GOOD.
SORRY, NOT BUYING THAT ONE. SEE YOU DOWNSTAIRS IN TEN MINUTES.

COURTNEY WRESTLED FOR THE STRENGTH TO RISE, BUT IT WAS NO USE. THANKFULLY, HER MOTHER SEEMED TO HAVE FORGOTTEN ABOUT HER.

BY EVENING, SHE SUMMONED ENOUGH STRENGTH TO GO DOWNSTAIRS. DINNER HAD BEEN EATEN, BUT SHE FOUND SOME LEFTOVERS IN THE KITCHEN.
STILL HUNGRY?

YOU LOOK AWFUL. MAYBE YOU ARE GETTING SICK.

I TRIED TO TELL YOU THIS MORNING.
YOU SHOULD PROBABLY STAY HOME TOMORROW.

THE NEXT MORNING SHE FELT EVEN WORSE. THIS TIME HER MOTHER DIDN'T BOTHER HER, AND ONCE AGAIN SHE SLEPT UNTIL EVENING.

SHE HAD NO APPETITE, BUT WORRIED ABOUT LOSING WHAT LITTLE STRENGTH SHE HAD LEFT.
SHE FORCED HERSELF TO TAKE THE LONG TREK DOWNSTAIRS.

HER FATHER WAS STILL AT THE DINNER TABLE, AS USUAL, READING THE WALL STREET JOURNAL AND PRETENDING TO UNDERSTAND IT.
HEY, HONEY.

YOU DON'T LOOK SO HOT. YOUR MOTHER SAID YOU WERE A LITTLE UNDER THE WEATHER LAST NIGHT.
YOU'RE DEFINITELY STAYING HOME TOMORROW.

THE UNSPOKEN THREAT OF A VISIT TO THE DOCTOR LOOMED MENACINGLY.
NO, NO, I'M OKAY.
SWEETIE, YOU'RE NEVER GOING TO GET BETTER IF YOU DON'T GET SOME REST.

THAT'S ABOUT ALL I'VE BEEN DOING.
WELL, CATHY KELLER'S MOM SAID YOU WERE OUT SHOPPING WITH THE GIRLS AFTER SCHOOL TODAY.

REALLY? DOES THAT SOUND LIKE ME?

GOOD POINT.

IT'S BEEN RATHER REFRESHING.
COME TO THINK OF IT, YOU REALLY HAVEN'T BEEN YOURSELF LATELY.

GEE, THANKS. CAN I EAT NOW?

DON'T OVERDO IT, DEAR. ISN'T THAT YOUR THIRD HELPING?
I KNEW ALL THAT PERFUME WOULD EVENTUALLY EAT AWAY HER BRAIN.

THE FOLLOWING MORNING, COURTNEY'S CONDITION STILL HADN'T IMPROVED. IF ANYTHING, SHE FELT WORSE THAN EVER. BUT FEAR OF DR. GRACE'S GHOULISH BEDSIDE MANNER SPURRED HER OUT OF BED.

I HAVE THE GRADES FOR YESTERDAY'S QUIZ. DON'T START CALLING HARVARD JUST YET, FOLKS.
Essay: Describe your last trip abroad
MRS. FINCH, WILL I BE ABLE TO TAKE A MAKEUP TEST?

DON'T BE SILLY. YOU DID GREAT.
WAY TO GO, COURTNEY.

GOOD JOB, MISS CRUMRIN. SEE WHAT YOU CAN DO WHEN YOU JUST APPLY YOURSELF?
YEAH. HEY, THANKS FOR HELPING ME OUT.
B+
COURTNEY, NEEDLESS TO SAY, WAS TOO PERPLEXED TO ANSWER.

I REALLY DON'T THINK I'M UP FOR RACKET-BALL TODAY.
DOESN'T SURPRISE ME. YOU'VE REALLY BEEN GOING FOR IT THESE LAST COUPLE OF DAYS.

I HAVE?
DON'T BE SO MODEST. OH, BY THE WAY, YOUR UNIFORM IS HERE.

UNIFORM?
SURE. I HAD TO PULL A FEW STRINGS TO GET YOU ON THE TEAM THIS LATE, BUT YOUR ENTHUSIASM IMPRESSED ME.
BARNARD
HILLSBOROUGH
54

I DON'T THINK ANYONE'S EVER SAID THAT TO ME BEFORE.
54

OF COURSE, IT WAS EASY TO WRITE OFF HER PARENTS' WEIRD BEHAVIOR AS BRAIN DAMAGE, BUT THIS WAS ANOTHER MATTER. HAD SHE GONE TO SCHOOL THE PREVIOUS DAY AND BEEN TOO SICK TO REMEMBER? IT DIDN'T MAKE SENSE.
YO! CRUMRIN!
HEY, COURTNEY.
HEY, GIRLFRIEND!
YOU COMING SHOPPING AGAIN TODAY?
MMMPH.
...GRUMBLE...
DESPITE HER GROWING CONFUSION, COURTNEY'S ENERGY SLOWLY DIMINISHED. BY LUNCHTIME, SHE COULD BARELY EAT.

AT LAST, EXHAUSTION OVERTOOK HER.

ZZZZZZZZZZZZZZZZZZZ...

SHE AWOKE HALF AN HOUR LATER, AND REALIZED SHE WAS LATE FOR CLASS.
BA!!
WA!?!

IT WAS ALL SHE COULD DO TO STRUGGLE BACK TO THE SCHOOLHOUSE.
JUST NOT MY WEEK.

ROOM 4
BUT WHAT SHE SAW THERE STOPPED HER COLD.
CAN SOMEONE TELL ME WHAT ABOUT THIS SENTENCE IS INCORRECT?
COURTNEY?

IT'S "MY AUNT, WITH WHOM I TRAVELED TO PARIS", NOT "WHO I TRAVELED TO PARIS WITH".
VERY GOOD. YOU'RE REALLY ON THE BALL TODAY, YOUNG LADY.

THANK YOU, MRS. FINCH.
COURTNEY HAD NEVER BEEN SO HORRIFIED AS SHE WAS THAT MOMENT. AND A SECOND LATER...

...HER HORROR DOUBLED.

IT WAS AS THOUGH HER DOPPELGANGER'S GAZE HAD REACHED OUT AND STOLE EVERY SPARE OUNCE OF HER STRENGTH.

SHE STAGGERED AWAY, WITH NO GOAL IN MIND BUT TO GET HOME.

IT TOOK HOURS.

SO THEN CATHY SAYS "GET WITH IT, BABE."

"MY DAD CAN BUY AND SELL YOU AND YOUR LITTLE STORE."
HA HAHA! THAT'S PRICELESS.

SO HER ATTITUDE SHAPED UP AFTER THAT.
OH YEAH, CATHY SAYS WE CAN COME TO HER PARENTS' COCKTAIL PARTY ON SUNDAY.
THAT'S GREAT, HONEY.
I ALWAYS SAID YOU'D MAKE FRIENDS IF YOU HAVE THE RIGHT ATTITUDE.

MOM? DAD?
I KNOW. YOU WERE RIGHT, AS ALWAYS.
I LOVE YOU, HONEY.

TERROR AND REVULSION MIXED PAINFULLY IN COURTNEY'S GUT.

WITNESSING THE EXCHANGE BETWEEN THE IMPOSTER AND HER FAMILY, SHE SUDDENLY SAW JUST HOW OUT OF PLACE SHE HAD ALWAYS BEEN.

IT HAD USURPED HER LIFE EFFORTLESSLY AND WAS WELCOMED BY EVERYONE WITHOUT QUESTION.
TREVOR
weenci
BUMPS
weenci
the weenci store
CONTEMPTO

AND WHY NOT?
WHAT REASON HAD THEY TO LIKE HER MORE THAN IT? WHAT DID SHE OFFER THE WORLD?

FOR ALL HER TRUE SELF MATTERED TO ANYONE...
...SHE MIGHT NEVER HAVE EXISTED AT ALL.

HEY.
I THINK IT'S TIME WE TALKED.
WHAT ARE YOU?

DUH! I'M YOU NOW, OBVIOUSLY.
I HAVE TO SAY, YOU DIDN'T MAKE THIS DIFFICULT.
YOU MIGHT AS WELL HAVE HANDED YOUR LIFE OVER ALL GIFT-WRAPPED.

GET...
OUT...
OH COME ON. YOU DON'T WANT THAT.

YOU WANT ME HERE.

YOU COULD NEVER BE THE PERSON THEY WANT. YOU DON'T HAVE IT IN YOU.

IT'S BETTER THIS WAY, FOR BOTH OF US.

I GET YOUR LIFE, AND YOUR MOM AND DAD, YOUR TEACHERS, YOUR CLASSMATES, EVERYONE GETS A COURTNEY THEY CAN LIKE.

AND YOU GET TO FINALLY FIT INTO THE WORLD. EVERYBODY WINS.

ADMIT IT. I'M MUCH BETTER AT BEING COURTNEY CRUMRIN THAN YOU EVER WERE.

WHAT THE HECK ARE YOU TALKING ABOUT?
YOU SUCK AT BEING ME!

WHAT!?!
LOOK AT YOU!
YOU DON'T LOOK LIKE ME, YOU DON'T TALK LIKE ME...

YOUR PARENTS SURE DIDN'T KNOW THE DIFFERENCE.
MY MOM WOULD KISS A DISEASED MOLLUSK IF IT COULD GET HER INTO A COCKTAIL PARTY.
THEY'RE BOTH SELFISH MORONS.

YOU HAVE NO FRIENDS. I MADE FRIENDS...
CATHY KELLER SAYS I'M COOL.

CONGRATS! YOU CAN KISS ASS. DON'T BREAK YOUR ARM PATTING YOURSELF ON THE BACK.
JUST THE FACT THAT YOUR LAME PERFORMANCE ACTUALLY FOOLED THESE PEOPLE SHOULD TELL YOU WHAT NITWITS THEY ARE.
WHAT DO YOU MEAN, LAME?

IF YOU WANTED TO BECOME COURTNEY CRUMRIN, YOU SHOULD HAVE DONE A LITTLE MORE HOMEWORK.
WAIT A MINUTE...
I'M RUDE, BAD-TEMPERED, AND BASICALLY, I DON'T LIKE PEOPLE.
MAYBE THAT MAKES ME A JERK, BUT IT SURE BEATS WHAT YOU ARE.
WHAT DO YOU THINK I AM?
A PHONY.
WHACK

SPUTT

OH BUGGER!

COURTNEY?

NICE TO SEE YOU. I HEARD YOU'D BEEN ILL.

NAH, I'M OKAY.
MAY I COME IN?

SURE...
SO YOU WERE ALRIGHT WHILE I WAS AWAY? NO DISASTERS?

I CAN TAKE CARE OF MYSELF, UNCLE A.
HMMM. SO IT WOULD SEEM.

BUT I KINDA MISSED YOU.

AND I YOU, LITTLE ONE.

YEH
STILL HANGIN'
ABOUT?

WELL,
THAT'S THE
STORY A' HOW
YOUNG COURTNEY
COME TO LIVE
IN CRUMRIN
HOUSE.

SHE AND OL' MAN CRUMRIN ARE THICK AS
THIEVES NOW. NEVER THOUGHT A LITTLE
BRAT LIKE 'ER COULD MELT 'IS ICY HEART.
THOUGH 'E TRIES TO
KEEP 'ER AWAY FROM
CERTAIN BOOKS.

'ER FOLKS'RE STILL TRYIN'
TE BE ALL POSH, FIT IN WITH
THE NEIGHBORHOOD GENTRY.
BLEAGH!
Fruitcake
MARK YEH, THEY
THINK "BOURGEOIS"
IS A BEDROOM.

BUT
EVERYONE'S
TUCKED IN THERE
ALL COZY NOW,
BLESS 'EM.

A'COURSE,
IT WON'T LAST. NOT
IN THIS NEIGHBORHOOD.
THERE'RE BAD THINGS
LURKIN' ABOUT.
WORSE
EVEN THEN
ME.

SO IF
YEH COME BACK
THIS WAY, WATCH
YER STEP.
YEH
AIN'T SEEN
NOTHING
YET.

Courtney Crumrin

Volume One

The Night Things

Bonus Material & Cover Gallery

Initial character sketches for *Courtney Crumrin and the Night Things*.

More of the original character designs for the debut issue of *Courtney Crumrin.*

Cover for Issue 1 of *Courtney Crumrin and the Night Things.*

Cover for Issue 2 of *Courtney Crumrin and the Night Things.*

Cover for Issue 3 of *Courtney Crumrin and the Night Things.*

Cover for Issue 4 of *Courtney Crumrin and the Night Things.*

Ted Naifeh

Ted Naifeh first appeared in the independent comics scene in 1999 as the artist for *Gloomcookie*, the goth romance comic he co-created with Serena Valentino for SLG Publishing. After a successful run, Ted decided to strike out on his own, writing and drawing *Courtney Crumrin and the Night Things*, a spooky children's fantasy series about a grumpy little girl and her adventures with her Warlock uncle.

Nominated for an Eisner Award for best limited series, Courtney Crumrin's success paved the way for *Polly and the Pirates*, another children's book, this time about a prim and proper girl kidnapped by pirates convinced she was the daughter of their long-lost queen.

Over the next few years, Ted wrote four volumes of *Courtney Crumrin*, plus a spin off book about her uncle. He also co-created *How Loathsome* with Tristan Crane, and illustrated two volumes of the videogame tie-in comic *Death Junior* with screenwriter Gary Whitta. More recently, he illustrated *The Good Neighbors*, a three volume graphic novel series written by *New York Times* best-selling author Holly Black, published by Scholastic.

In 2011, Ted wrote the sequel to *Polly and the Pirates*, and illustrated several *Batman* short stories for DC Comics. He is currently writing and illustrating the ongoing *Courtney Crumrin* series, which will celebrate its 10th year in 2012.

Ted lives in San Francisco, because he likes dreary weather.

Forbidden Magic